Paleo

Dessert Recipes

Delicious Cookies, Brownies & Bars, Ice Cream & Pudding, Cakes & Cupcakes, and Red Velvet & Coconut Frosting Cupcakes!

Contents

About the Book

This a helpful book for followers of the Paleo Diet. Whether you are new to the diet, or have been following the plan for years these recipes are worth a try. Enjoy healthy eating with these Paleo approved versions of indulgent desserts. The book starts with a variety of cookie recipes, then includes brownies and bars, ice cream and pudding and lastly cupcakes and cakes. Experiment and find your favorite Paleo desserts!

Introduction

The Paleo diet is short for Paleolithic which refers to the era before the development of agriculture. During this time, the people ate what was found in the natural environment including fruits, vegetables, meat, seafood and nuts. This diet is also sometimes called the caveman diet and consists of what can be naturally hunted or gathered. The diet is founded on the theory that the human body is better adapted to ingesting and using these foods rather than the typical modern day diet. Refined carbohydrates, sugars, dairy, wheat, processed foods and chemically changed foods are excluded. By eating to naturally found whole foods, research has found a reduction in many diseases as well as weight loss.

The foods included in the Paleo diet plan can be delicious and are very nutrient dense. Within this book, find creative recipes using Paleo approved ingredients to make some of the most delicious dessert recipes. Eat your way to health and still enjoy your sweet tooth indulgence with these desserts.

Cookies

Chocolate Chip Cookies

Serves 12

¾ C. almond flour (packed)

1 tbsp. coconut flour

1 large organic egg

1 tbsp. raw honey

½ tsp. vanilla extract

½ tsp. baking powder

1 tbsp. melted coconut oil

2 tbsp. whole almond milk (unsweetened)

3 tbsp. dark chocolate chips (nondairy)

Begin by preheating your oven to 350 degrees. Then prepare a baking sheet by lightly oiling with coconut oil. Next use a medium sized bowl to combine your coconut and almond flour with the baking powder and stirring well. Now mix in your wet ingredients to the dry flour mix and blend thoroughly to form cookie dough. Split your dough into a dozen equal balls and place on the prepped cookie sheet. Place your cookies in the oven to bake for ten minutes, let cool and serve.

Coconut Pecan Cookies

Serves 12

1½ c. almond flour (packed)

3 tbsp. coconut flour

¾ tsp. baking soda

½ tsp. sea salt

2 tbsp. raw palm sugar

4 tbsp. melted coconut oil

2 large eggs (beaten)

4 tbsp. raw honey

2 tsp. vanilla extract

1 c. pecans (chopped)

¼ c. whole pumpkin seeds

1 c. coconut flakes (unsweetened)

Begin by heating your oven to 325 degrees. Next prepare a large baking sheet by lightly oiling with coconut oil, or lining with parchment paper. Then in a large bowl, combine your flours, baking soda, salt and palm sugar and mix well. Now add in your shortening, honey, vanilla and eggs and mix thoroughly. When dough has formed, add in the coconut flakes, pecans and pumpkin seeds and stir until evenly distributed. Separate your dough into twelve equal sized balls and set them on you baking sheet. Place your cookies into the oven and bake for ten to fifteen minutes, being sure to check for burning often. Place on a cooling rack for another fifteen minutes before serving.

Almond Butter Cookies

Serves 12

1 c. almond butter

⅓ c. raw honey

1 large egg

1½ tsp. baking soda

2 tbsp. coconut flour

¼ c. raw dark chocolate

Begin by preheating your oven to 350 degrees. Next in a large mixing bowl, add in the eggs, butter, honey and baking soda and blend thoroughly. Now stir in your coconut flour and chocolate and finish mixing. Roll your dough into twelve equal sized balls and space them evenly on a lightly oiled baking sheet. Flatten each ball slightly with a fork and then place in the oven to bake for ten minutes. Cool on a rack for fifteen minutes and serve.

Funky Monkey Cookies

Serves 12

1 c. almond butter

¼ c. raw honey

1 large egg

½ c. mashed banana (very ripe)

2 tbsp. hazelnut butter (chocolate)

1 tsp. vanilla extract

1 tbsp. ground cinnamon

½ tsp. baking powder

½ tsp. baking soda

½ c. pecans (chopped)

½ c. raw dark chocolate

Pinch of salt

Start by preheating your oven to 350 degrees. Gather a large mixing bowl, place all of your ingredients inside and mix thoroughly to form dough. Next, lightly oil a baking sheet with coconut oil and place the cookie dough on top in twelve equally sized balls. Place in the oven to bake for thirteen minutes, cool and serve.

Banana Apple Cookies w/ Walnuts

Serves 20

2 ripe bananas

1 red apple

1/3 c. almond butter

1/3 c. whole coconut milk

1/3 c. coconut flour (sifted)

1/3 c. walnuts (chopped)

½ tsp. baking soda

1 tbsp. ground cinnamon

Begin by preheating your oven to 250 degrees. Then, cover two baking sheets in a light coat of coconut oil or parchment. While the oven warms, combine all your ingredients in a large mixing bowl (except the banana, walnuts and apples) and stir well. Place the apples, banana and walnuts in your food processor and pulse until lightly pureed. Place the fruit and nut puree in with your dough and mix thoroughly. Spoon equally sized mounds of dough onto the prepared baking sheet and bake for twenty five minutes. Enjoy!

Lime & Coconut Cookies

Serves 15

2 large eggs

2 limes (zest)

1 tbsp. melted coconut oil

¼ c. whole coconut milk

2/3 c. raw honey

1 c. shredded coconut (unsweetened)

3 tbsp. coconut flour

Begin by preheating your oven to 350 degrees and lining a baking sheet with a light coat of coconut oil. Then combine all of your dry ingredients together in a large bowl and stir thoroughly. In a separate mixing bowl, combine all of your wet ingredients and whisk to combine. Add your wet and dry mixes together and mix well to form dough. Spoon your cookie dough onto the baking sheet and place in the oven for fifteen minutes. Let cool on the rack for about ten minutes before serving.

Paleo Vanilla Cookies

Serves 6

2 c. almond flour

1 tsp. vanilla extract

¼ tsp. sea salt

¼ tsp. baking soda

2 tbsp. raw maple syrup (or honey)

2 tbsp. melted coconut oil

2 large eggs

2 oz. raw dark organic (broke into pieces)

Begin by preheating your oven to 325 degrees and lining a cookie sheet with parchment or coconut oil. Gather two bowls, one for your wet ingredients and one for your dry ingredients and mix each thoroughly. When both are done mixing, add the wet mix to the dry and stir again to form dough. Separate the dough into equal sized dough balls and place on the cookie sheet. Flatten each ball slightly and place in the oven to bake for fifteen minutes. Cool and serve.

Brownies & Bars

Fudge Brownies

Serves 10

1 c. almond butter

½ c. whole coconut milk

2 large eggs

2 tsp. vanilla extract

¼ tsp. sea salt

1/3 c. raw cocoa powder

¼ c. raw palm sugar

1/3 c. raw dark chocolate

1/3 c. walnuts (chopped)

Start by preheating your oven to 350 degrees. Then lightly grease a baking dish (8x8) with coconut oil and set to the side for later on. In a large mixing bowl, whisk your coconut milk, eggs, almond butter, salt and vanilla together. When thoroughly whisked, add in your chocolate, sugar and cocoa powder and stir well. Pour your finished batter into the baking dish and evenly top with chopped walnuts. Place in the oven to bake for fifteen to twenty minutes. Let cool and serve.

Beet Brownie

Serves 10

5 oz. raw dark chocolate

¼ c. melted coconut oil

⅓ c. raw honey

2 medium eggs

2 tsp. vanilla extract

¼ tsp. almond extract

1 c. almond flour

2 tbsp. coconut flour

¼ c. raw cocoa powder (unsweetened)

1½ tsp. baking soda

¼ tsp. sea salt

2 beets (cooked and pureed)

Begin by setting your oven to 350 degrees to preheat. Next, grease and 8x8 baking dish and lightly dust with almond flour. Now melt your chocolate, coconut oil and honey in a sauce pan on low heat and thoroughly mix. Combine your eggs, almond extract and vanilla together in a mixing bowl and then stir in the chocolate mix. Use a separate bowl to whisk all of your dry ingredients together and then pour in the wet mix. When your wet and dry mixes are fully incorporated, mix in the pureed beets and stir well. Pour the batter into the prepared baking pan and bake for twenty five minutes. Cool and serve.

Raspberry Date Chocolate Bars

Serves 9

2 ripe bananas

¼ c. raspberries

12 dates (pitted)

¾ c. raw cocoa (unsweetened)

½ c. almonds (chopped)

½ c. walnuts (chopped)

5 tbsp. almond butter

5 tbsp. raw honey

Begin by throwing your walnuts, almonds, dates, cocoa powder into a food processor and puree for five minutes until a smooth paste is reached. Place the processed paste into the bottom of a baking dish and spread evenly. Next place the raspberries, almond butter, honey and bananas in the processor and puree for five minutes as well. Pour this mix into the baking pan, covering the first mix and then place in the freezer for two hours to set. Cut into bars and serve.

Sweet Potato Brownies

Serves 16

1 avocado

1 c. sweet potato (pureed)

½ c. natural apple sauce (unsweetened)

¼ c. date paste

1 tsp. vanilla extract

4 medium eggs

¼ c. coconut flour (packed)

2 tbsp. arrowroot flour

½ c. raw cacao powder (unsweetened)

1 tsp. ancho chili (dried and chopped)

½ tsp. sea salt

1 tsp. baking soda

½ c. pecans (chopped)

Icing

¼ c. date paste

½ c. hazelnut butter

¼ c. raw cacao powder (unsweetened)

2 tbsp. raw honey

½ c. whole coconut milk

Dash sea salt

Begin by preheating your oven to 375 degrees and greasing a 8x8 baking pan with coconut oil. Next use a food processor to puree the sweet potato, avocado, applesauce, vanilla and date paste until smooth. When done pureeing, stir in the cacao powder, and mix well. Now add in each egg one at a time and puree between each one. Gather a large mixing bowl and add in all of your dry ingredients, then whisk to incorporate. Add your dry mix and pecans to the wet mix in the processor and puree until smooth. Pour your batter into the pan from earlier and bake at 350 degrees for twenty five minutes. When done baking, place on a cooling rack for twenty minutes and then into the refrigerator for an hour. As your brownies cool you can begin to prepare the icing. Place all of your ingredients for the icing into the food processor and puree on high until a creamy consistency is reached. Remove the brownies from the fridge and spread the frosting evenly over the top. Return the brownies to the fridge for a full eight hours to fully set, then cut into squares and enjoy!

Chewy Chocolate Chip Granola Bars

Serves 8-10

1½ c. almonds (sliced thin)

2 c. shredded coconut (unsweetened)

1/3 c. sunflower kernels

1/3 c. pumpkin seeds (shelled)

1 tbsp. sesame seeds

½ c. almond flower (sifted)

1/3 c. melted coconut oil

¼ c. almond butter (unsweetened)

¼ c. raw honey

1 tsp. vanilla extract

¾ tsp. baking soda

1 tbsp. flax meal

1½ tbsp. water (filtered)

¾ c. dried apricots (chopped)

Start by preheating your oven to 325 degrees and also lightly oiling a 9x13 baking pan. Set your prepared pan to the side and then mix your flax seed meal with water and set that to the side as well. Next put your pumpkin seeds in a food processor and pulse to break into small pieces. Now get your flax/water mix and stir in the honey, coconut oil, vanilla and honey and blend well. Add in the baking soda and baking flour and mix thoroughly until smooth and even. Place the remaining ingredients into flax meal mix and stir thoroughly, then pour the batter into baking pan. Put the baking pan in the oven and let bake for twenty five minutes. When they are done baking, let them cool for about fifteen minutes and then refrigerate for an hour before cutting into squares.

Chocolate Cherry Granola Bars

Serves 10

2½ c. mixed nuts (unsalted)

½ c. raw dark chocolate

½ c. dried cherries

2 tbsp. melted coconut oil

1 tbsp. vanilla extract

1/3 c. raw honey

4 tbsp. coconut nectar

¼ tsp. sea salt

Begin by lining an 8x8 baking pan with parchment and then setting your oven to 300 degrees to heat up. Next place your nuts in a food processor and pulse to make granola sized chunks. Now add the cherries, chocolate and salt to the chopped nuts and pulse a few more times to mix well. Set the mix to the side and then heat a sauce pan on medium heat on the stove top. Add in the coconut nectar, oil and vanilla extract and bring to a boil while constantly whisking. Pour the contents of the sauce pan into your nut mixture and mix evenly. Place the mix into your baking pan and press down firmly with a spatula, then, place in the oven to bake for a half hour. Remove from the heat and cool for an hour before cutting and serving.

Bird Bars

Serves 16

1 c. almond flour

¼ tsp. sea salt

¼ c. melted coconut oil

2 tbsp. raw honey

1 tbsp. water (filtered)

1 tsp. vanilla extract

½ c. shredded coconut (unsweetened)

½ c. pumpkin seeds

½ c. sunflower kernels

¼ c. slivered almonds (chopped)

¼ c. raisins

Begin by preheating your oven to 350 degrees. Then use a food processor to puree the, almond flour, coconut oil, salt, water, vanilla and honey together. When smooth, add in your nuts, raisins and seeds and pulse again until smooth. Pour the dough into an 8x8 baking dish and press down firmly with your hands. Place the dish into the oven and bake for twenty minutes. Once the time is up, remove from heat and let cool and set for three hours. Cut to bars and enjoy!

Cranberry Granola Bars

Serves 10

3 c. raw mixed nuts (unsalted)

1 c. dried cranberries

2 c. shredded coconut (unsweetened)

¼ c. melted coconut oil

½ c. almond butter

½ c. raw honey

¼ tsp. vanilla extract

½ tsp. sea salt

1 tsp. ground cinnamon

Begin by lining a 9x13 baking dish with a light coat of oil and parchment paper, then set to the side. Combine your seeds and nuts in a large bowl and mix well. Pour the nut and seed mix into a food processor and pulse to tiny pieces. Stir your shredded coconut and cranberries into the seed and nut mix and blend well. Next set your mix to the side and put a small sauce pan on medium heat. Add in the butter, honey, salt, coconut oil, vanilla and cinnamon and cook for five minutes, beings sure to stir constantly. Mix your honey butter sauce into the dry mix and combine thoroughly. Place the mix into your pan and cover with parchment paper, then press down firmly to help set the mixture. Now let the bars settle on the counter top for a few hours and then finish up in the freezer for an hour. Cut to bars and enjoy.

Ice Cream & Pudding

Lavender Blueberry Ice Cream

Serves 3-4

1 c. blueberries (fresh or frozen)

¼ c. raw honey

1 tsp. vanilla extract

1 tbsp. lavender buds (fine ground)

Pinch of sea salt

For the ice cream

2 c. whole coconut milk

⅓ c. raw honey

1 tsp. almond extract

Begin by heating your honey and blueberries in a sauce pan on medium heat, let cook until you have a thick jam like sauce. Now pour in the salt, vanilla and lavender and stir well while continuing to cook for five more minutes. When done, set your sauce to the side in the refrigerator for later. In a large mixing bowl, whisk your ice cream ingredients together and pour the mix into your ice cream maker. Let the mix churn until it starts to become thick and then pour in the jam and continue churning until the ice cream is firm. Store in the freezer.

Chocolate Almond Butter Ice Cream

Serves 2-3

2 c. whole coconut milk

¼ c. raw honey

¼ c. almond butter

2 tbs. raw cocoa powder (unsweetened)

1 tsp. vanilla extract

1 tsp. ground cinnamon

Start off by putting your ingredients in a blender and blending on high for one minute, then pour into your ice cream maker. Set on medium speed and churn for a half hour. Store in the freezer.

Strawberry Ice Cream

Serves 6

Syrup

2 c. strawberries (fresh)

1 tbsp. raw honey (or maple syrup)

3 tbsp. water (filtered)

1 tbsp. balsamic vinegar

Pinch of salt

For the ice cream base:

2 c. whole coconut milk

2 c. low fat coconut milk

½ c. raw honey (or maple syrup)

1 tsp. vanilla extract

Begin by making the syrup; heat a sauce pan on medium heat and place in the strawberries. Next, pour in the remaining sauce ingredients and cook for about ten minutes, being sure to stir often. When the strawberries begin to break down, pour into a food processor and blend smooth. Then place your syrup in the freezer to cool while you make the ice cream. Whisk your remaining ingredients together in a mixing bowl until smooth and well blended, then transfer to your ice cream maker. Let churn for fifteen minutes and then pour the syrup in and continue to churn for another fifteen minutes. Store in the freezer.

Cookie Dough Ice Cream

Serves 6

1 batch of Paleo cookie dough (broke to small pieces)

3 c. whole coconut milk

½ c. raw maple syrup

Pinch of sea salt

1 tbsp. vanilla extract

Start this super easy recipe by whisking everything except the cookie dough together in a large bowl. When done whisking, pour your mix into an ice cream maker and let churn for half an hour. Once the ice cream has frozen stir in the cookie dough pieces, serve and store the leftovers in the freezer.

Yogurt Gelato

Serves 2-3

½ c. whole coconut milk

½ c. heavy coconut cream

½ c. raw honey

2 c. whole yogurt (unsweetened)

Begin by heating your honey, coconut milk and cream on medium heat in a large sauce pan. Cook for five minutes, stirring constantly, and then set in the fridge to cool for ten minutes. When cool, stir in the yogurt until smooth, then pour into your ice cream maker and churn for twenty five minutes until firm. Store in the freezer.

Banana Chocolate Pudding

Serves 4-6

1½ c. whole coconut milk

4 tbsp. raw honey

1 tsp. vanilla extract

1 large bananas (very ripe and mashed)

2 tbsp. raw cacao powder (unsweetened)

Begin by refrigerating your coconut milk for eight hours to separate the cream from the liquid. Scrape out the cream once it has separated and put it in a mixing bowl, you can either save or toss the liquid. Next whip in the cream, honey and vanilla until nice and fluffy and then add in your mashed banana and cacao powder and blend well. Let chill in the fridge for an hour and then serve with some cacao powder sprinkled on top.

Very Berry Ice Cream

Serves 5

¾ c. raspberries (fresh or frozen)

¾ c. strawberries (fresh or frozen)

1½ c. whole coconut milk

½ tsp. vanilla extract

2 tbsp. raw honey

1 tsp. lemon juice (fresh squeezed)

2 large eggs (whisked)

1/8 tsp. sea salt

Begin by pureeing your berries in a food processor until they have completely broken down, then set to the side for later. Gather a large sauce pan, heat on medium heat and pour in the vanilla and coconut milk. Whisk continually for five minutes and then turn the heat off and let cool for another five minutes. Once the mix has cooled a bit, stir in your eggs and whisk rapidly until smooth. Now add your mixture to a large bowl and stir in the berry puree. Add in the honey, salt and lemon juice and stir again until well incorporated. Cover up the top of your bowl and place in the refrigerator for six hours, then place in an ice cream maker to churn for half an hour. Store leftovers in the freezer.

Cakes & Cupcakes

Chocolate and Almond Butter Cupcakes

8 Servings

¼ c. sifted coconut flour

3 eggs (whisked)

¼ c. cacao powder (100%)

1/3 c. honey

¼ c. coconut oil

½ tsp. sifted baking soda

1 tsp. pure vanilla extract

Salt to taste

Almond Butter Topping:

¾ c. almond butter

¾ c. palm shortening

1/3 c. honey

2 tsp. pure vanilla extract

Salt to taste

Heat the oven to 350 and line a muffin tin with cupcake liners. Combine the almond butter and shortening and beat until it becomes light and airy. Slowly mix in the salt, 2 tsp. vanilla and 1/3 c. honey. Once thoroughly combined, set aside. In a medium bowl mic the baking soda, salt, cacao and flour well in another bowl combine the eggs, vanilla, oil and honey until the eggs are frothy and the ingredients are well mixed. Then slowly stir the egg mixture into the flour bowl and beat until smooth. Divide between the cupcake liners and bake for 16 minutes. After they cool spread the almond butter topping on each one and enjoy!

Chocolate Covered Strawberries Cupcake Style

6 Servings

1 ¾ c. sifted almond flour

2 tsp. baking soda

1 tbsp. cacao powder (raw 100%)

¼ c. chocolate chips (Enjoy life Brand)

1 large egg

2 tbsp. melted coconut oil

½ c. full fat coconut milk

1 tbsp. honey

Handful of fresh strawberries

Chocolate Dipping:

6 tbsp. full fat coconut milk

¾ c. chocolate chips (Enjoy Life Brand)

Preheat the oven to 350 degrees and line each tin with a paper liner. Combine the flour, cacao and baking soda together until well combined. In a double boiler add the ¼ c. of chocolate chips and melt them down. Once melted let them cool for a few minutes then add in the egg, oil, honey and milk and stir until smooth. Slowly stir in the flour mixture and stir until smooth and fully incorporated. Cut the greens off of 6 strawberries. Divide the cupcake mixture between the 6 cupcake cups. Place a strawberry in each cup, pointing down. Bake for 20 minutes then let them cool down. While cooling melt the ¾ c. of chocolate chips then stir in the milk. Stir until smooth then lather on each cooled cupcake. Enjoy!

Mini Pumpkin Pie Cupcakes

12 Servings

1 c. pumpkin

¼ c. raw honey

2 large eggs

Ground cinnamon to taste

1 tsp. baking soda and powder

Nutmeg to taste

½ c. almond butter

1 tsp. vanilla extract

Heat up the oven to 350 degrees and line 12 muffin cups with paper liners. Mix the butter well until fluffy, then stir in the honey, eggs, vanilla then pumpkin. Once smooth add in the cinnamon and nutmeg to taste. Then divide, the batter between the 12 paper liners. Bake 30 minutes then serve.

Red Velvet with Coconut Frosting Cupcakes

Servings

2 large eggs

2 ½ c. fine almond meal

½ c. melted coconut oil

½ c. raw honey

1 ½ tbsp. pure vanilla extract

Sea salt to taste

3 tsp. raw cocoa powder

2 tbsp. beet juice

Heat up the oven to 350 degrees and add the paper liners into the muffin tins. In a medium bowl, combine the eggs until frothy and well combined. Then add in the honey, oil and vanilla. In another bowl combine the almond meal, powder and salt. Then slowly stir the flour mixture into the egg mixture. Once well combined, add in the beet juice and combine thoroughly until batter turns red. Then divide it between the 12 cups and bake 20 minutes. Serve topped with your this coconut frosting.

Coconut Frosting:

13.5 oz. coconut milk (full fat)

1 tsp. pure vanilla extract

Refrigerate the can of milk and remove the cream that forms on the top. Mix that with the vanilla then spread on each cupcake.

Vanilla Cupcakes

7 Servings

½ c. sifted coconut flour + 2 tbsp.

½ tsp. salt

¼ tsp. sifted baking soda

4 large eggs

1/3 c. fat (olive oil)

½ c. raw honey

1 tbsp. pure vanilla

Heat up the oven to 350 and add paper liners into a muffin tin. Combine the dry ingredients together in one bowl and the wet ingredients in a separate bowl. Mix until smooth separately. Slowly stir the flour mixture into the egg mixture until a nice smooth batter forms. Then divide between the muffin cups and bake for about 20 minutes. Top with the coconut milk recipe above.

Watermelon Cake

Serves 6-8

1 seedless watermelon

4 c. whole coconut milk (refrigerated for eight hours)

½ tsp. vanilla extract

1 tbsp. raw honey (maple syrup works, but honey is better suited)

1 c. shredded coconut (unsweetened)

Favorite fresh fruit (for topping)

Start by making the coconut whipped cream; after refrigerating, remove the coconut cream from the liquid with a spoon and discard the liquid. Stir in the honey and vanilla and whip by had until the cream is nice and fluffy. Place in the fridge to cool for later. Next, use a skillet on high heat to toast your shredded coconut until lightly browned and then remove from the heat. Now chop the top and bottom from your watermelon and remove the rind from the leftover section. Then coat in whipped coconut cream and shredded coconut. Cut into slices and top with fresh fruit before serving.

Paleo Lemon Pound Cake

Serves 12

2 c. almond flour (sifted)

½ c. coconut flour (sifted)

½ tsp. sea salt

1 tsp. baking soda

2/3 c. raw honey

2/3 c. melted coconut oil

4 medium eggs

½ c. whole coconut milk

2 tbsp. raw lemon extract

1 tbsp. fresh lemon zest

Begin by preheating your oven to 350 degrees and the lightly oiling a 9x9 baking dish with coconut oil. Combine all of your dry ingredients in a large bowl and whisk thoroughly. Next place your eggs, coconut milk, honey, coconut oil, lemon extract and zest into a food processor and pureeing for three minutes until completely smooth. Pour your wet mix into your dry mix and stir until thoroughly combined. Fill your baking dish with the batter and place in the oven to bake for thirty to forty minutes. Let cool for ten minutes and serve.

Carrot Cake

Serves 12

5 large carrots (peeled and shredded)

1 c. raw maple syrup

¾ c. coconut flour (sifted)

1 tbsp. cinnamon (ground)

1 tsp. baking soda

1 tsp. sea salt

10 large eggs

10 dates

1 tbsp. vanilla extract

1 c. melted coconut oil

Begin by placing your shredded carrots in a large bag or Tupperware and cover in maple syrup, then place in the refrigerator for an hour to soak. Next set your oven to 325 degrees while you prepare the cake mix. Use a small mixing bowl to whisk all your dry ingredients together. Add the dates, eggs, coconut oil and vanilla to a food processor and puree for two minutes until smooth. Now add your dry ingredients to the processor and puree again until smooth. Remove your carrots from the bag and stir them into the cake batter, then pour your batter into two 9x9 cake pans. Place in the oven to bake for twenty five minutes, then cut and serve warm with a bit of coconut butter.

Fudge Cake

Serves 6

18 oz. raw dark chocolate (broke to small pieces)

1 c. coconut oil

½ c. raw maple syrup (or raw honey)

¼ tsp. sea salt

6 large eggs

Begin by melting your coconut oil and dark chocolate together in a sauce pan on low heat. Once the oil and chocolate has melted, stir in the maple syrup and salt. One by one, beat in all six eggs until smooth. Next grease a shallow round baking dish with coconut oil, then dust with powdered cocoa powder and pour in the batter. Bake in the oven at 275 degrees for an hour and then let cool for two more hours. Cut and serve with a dab of coconut cream on top.

Made in the USA
Middletown, DE
01 November 2021